How to Build Your Writer's Platform

INTERNET MARKETING 101 FOR WRITERS

GEOFF HUGHES

Madhouse Media Publishing
Port Macquarie, NSW, Australia

Copyright © 2020 by Geoff Hughes

All rights reserved. No part of this publication may be reproduced, distributed or transmitted in any form or by any means, including photocopying, recording, or other electronic or mechanical methods, without the prior written permission of the publisher, except in the case of brief quotations embodied in critical reviews and certain other noncommercial uses permitted by copyright law. For permission requests, write to the publisher, addressed "Attention: Permissions Coordinator," at the address below:

Madhouse Media Publishing
PO Box 987
Port Macquarie
NSW 2444 Australia
www.madhousemedia.com.au

How to Build Your Writer's Platform / Geoff Hughes —1st ed.

ISBN 978-0-9925713-5-1

Contents

Forward 4
What is a Writer's Platform? 6
Why You Should Build Your Writer's Platform 9
The Uncomfortable Truth About Self-Publishing 11
The Rights and Wrongs of Self-Publishing 14
Setting Your Self-Publishing Goals 17
Making It All Happen 21
The Power of Blogging 24
Getting Social 28
Using Podcasts to Promote Your Book 34
Building Your Writer's Blog and Website 38
Why You Need to Grow a Mailing List 43
The End of the Beginning... 50
Marketing Resources 53
Free Tools 55
About the Author 58

This book is dedicated to creative self-published authors everywhere.

I love deadlines. I like the whooshing sound they make as they fly by...

—Douglas Adams

CHAPTER 1

Forward

Self-publishing a book is a big risk. It can also be a creative and satisfying way to take control of your writing career.

There are some amazing success stories about self-published writers who have seized on self-publishing as a means to get their work in front of readers. I'm inspired by writers like Hugh Howey (author of the WOOL series) and Joanna Penn (who writes supernatural thrillers as J.R. Penn, and books on how to self-publish under her real name).

These writers prove to me the power of self-publishing.

There are many other writers who channelled determination after rejection to find an audience by self-publishing. But this isn't another 'how to' book about self-publishing. It's about what comes next. It tells you how to maximise your chances of self-publishing success by connecting with your audience.

Let's not get too romantic about this. There are thousands of writers who have had little to no success with self-publishing. That's because selling books is a tough business and selling self-published books is a very tough business.

If you look closely at successful self-published authors, you'll notice they have one thing in common. They've all carefully built and curated a writer's platform to promote their books.

That's because building a writer's platform is the most important thing you can do to improve your chances of selling books.

Cost doesn't need to be a barrier. This book shows you how to get started using free online tools. The only real cost is your time.

If you are determined to build a career at writing and self-publishing (and it is possible), you will need a platform to promote your brand.

I'm going to show you it's not rocket science. If you have basic computer skills, you can put together your platform using established internet marketing techniques.

That's why the subtitle is Internet Marketing 101 for Writers. You need to understand how these techniques can help you build your platform.

So, I wrote this book to get you started on this important marketing task.

Let's go!

Geoff Hughes
Madhouse Media Publishing

CHAPTER 2

What is a Writer's Platform?

This book tells you how to build your writer's platform at close to zero cost. If you are lucky enough to sign to a bricks and mortar publisher, you won't need to worry about building a platform because you'll have the might of their marketing dollars promoting you and your book.

But then what happens when you sign up? Who owns your readers? How can you sustain a direct relationship with your readers if you're booted off your publisher's platform? These are questions all authors should think about. The entire reason to build and maintain your own platform - despite traditional versus self-publishing success - is to grow and maintain a direct channel to your readers.

And while an independent writer's platform can benefit traditionally published authors, it is critically important for self-published authors. You won't have the marketing expertise of a large publishing brand to help you. You'll need to do it all yourself.

This is both daunting and liberating. By curating your own platform, you alone control your relationship with your readers (and their email addresses).

A writer's platform lets you:

- Build a direct relationship with your readers
- Create a mailing list of your readers
- Create a direct sales channel for your readers
- Find beta readers
- Ask your readers directly for reviews

- Control your own marketing and distribution (even if you move from self-publishing to traditional publishing).

The key elements of a writer's platform are really quite simple. Let's go through the basics:

- A blog
- A mailing list
- A way for readers to join your mailing list
- A social media presence (Twitter, Facebook, Instagram, LinkedIn)
- A consistent, professional brand.

Putting all this together will give your platform a marketing advantage.

In this book, I'm going to help you break down your platform building into a simple three month project. Let's have a quick look.

MONTH 1: You'll map out and create your free Wordpress (wordpress.com) blog. If you can spare 20 minutes a day you can easily get this together in 30 days. That includes creating the blog, tweaking the template design, writing the copy for your 'About me' page (and book download page if you already have some work to share) and, importantly, your very first blog post.

You see, when you get started, no-one is going to start suddenly reading your blog . What happens is a slow build. As you write more content and promote more posts and get more follows and likes, you'll slowly increase your blog traffic and grow your mailing list.

So it doesn't really matter if you launch your blog and it's imperfect. The aim of the platform building game is to get parts of your platform ready enough to launch. You can easily tweak them as you go. A website is a 'live' document. You can always tweak it. Close enough is good enough. Think of the 90/10 rule. 90% is good enough to launch. You can tweak the 10% after launch. Make sure you have your Mailchimp (mailchimp.com) account set up and your sign-up form working before you launch. You want to maximise the opportunity to capture email addresses and build your list from the very beginning. The (90/10) rule also applies to Mailchimp. You'll have plenty of time to tweak email copy and form design once the basic elements are in place and the auto-responder is working.

MONTH 2: Get your social media pages up and running. Remember to cross-link from your social media pages to your blog. Keep your branding consistent. If you do your blog first, this is simple as you'll just be using the blog design on your social accounts. Follow the same 90/10 rule. Give yourself 30 days to create these accounts. Use Canva (canva.com) to create your header art. You can just resize the header art you have already created for your blog. Remember you must keep your brand consistent on every element of your platform.

MONTH 3: This is where it starts to happen. By now you should have your blog and social accounts linked up and brand consistent. For the final month, your task is to create a social media and blog publishing strategy map. Find some useful articles to share to your audience. Write a few original posts about you and your work as well. You can use Canva to create the art and a free scheduling tool like Buffer (buffer.com) or Hootsuite (hootsuite.com) to automatically schedule a drum beat of social media posts. To attract new readers, research appropriate hashtags for your posts and make sure every post has a link back to your blog.

> TIP: Use the free scheduling tool listed in the Free Tools chapter at the end of this book.

That's it! In three short months, you'll have a platform that's 90% great. You can now devote your 20 minutes a day to tweaking the remaining 10% of your platform and working on your blog and media schedule.

If you follow the tips in this book, you can build a basic writer's platform for free. As your needs and expertise grow, you can always upgrade. The important takeaway is that you've taken action. You haven't thought about creating your writer's platform, you've actually built one!

CHAPTER 3

Why You Should Build Your Writer's Platform

Let's imagine you're at a party with a bunch of shouty writers. You're shouting because there is free food and wine. And you're shouting to get the attention of readers who are drifting in and out of the party.

If it's a fancy party, you're also shouting to get the attention of a commissioning editor before she drinks too much free chardonnay and decides to go to a better party.

'Read me!'

'No me!'

'No, you must read MY staggering work of heartbreaking genius!'

How does anyone hear just one voice in all that noise? Now, let's imagine you are the only writer in that little bacchanal who had a small stage. With maybe a few LED theatre lights and a nice little PA system. Clipped to your collar is a radio microphone. Maybe you could get really fancy and have a cool video backdrop. Where do you think the attention of the room, of your potential readers, of the slightly drunk commissioning editor would focus?

That, in a nutshell, is what a writer's platform does for you. It lets you stand above the throng. To be heard. It helps you to gather an audience, and build your tribe. To engage future readers on your writer's journey and convert them to avid buyers and fans. And maybe, your platform will even get the attention of the commissioning editor.

I know, I know. 'I don't have the time to build a platform when I'm trying to write a book, juggle a career, raise a family.' That's a fair call.

If you're serious about a career as an independent author/publisher it's time worth investing because in this crowded media age, it's just not enough to just write your book, upload it to Smashwords or KDP and press Publish.

It's a satisfying thing, that initial 'published' rush, but after a few days you'll also realise (if you haven't already) that without a strategy, it's also futile.

If you don't market yourself and your book, you are just writing for yourself. You need to create an audience.

In the next chapter, I'll talk about the real truth of self-publishing.

CHAPTER 4

The Uncomfortable Truth About Self-Publishing

Let's talk about the elephant in the room. Most self-published books will fail. Not because they are bad. Not because of lazy content, story or grammar. They'll fail simply because there are already millions of self-published books on the market.

So how does any new writer have a chance of breaking through? It seems an impossible task, but if you check out any successful self-published author you'll discover they follow two simple rules.

First, they ensure their self-published masterpiece is professionally produced. Second, they understand that marketing is the key to growing an audience. One reason self-publishing gets a bad rap is because some writers don't ask for professional help. They either don't treat their work seriously enough, or just can't let go.

The phrase 'self-publishing' does not mean you do everything yourself. Just as serious writers treat their art seriously, amateurs take the opposite approach. Look deeper and you'll find these two simple rules which amateurs seem to unconsciously embrace. First, they'll take the 'self' in self-publishing literally. Second, they'll have no marketing or launch plan.

Releasing a largely unedited first draft, running it through a spell checker, designing your own cover and uploading the resulting 'frankenbook' to Amazon KDP is not self-publishing. It is a formula that will guarantee you'll have a very short self-publishing career.

You have to respect your art. If you don't, who else will? Good art always takes time. Good art pays attention to the details. Good art doesn't happen in a first draft. Sometimes good art requires investment. The eBook revolution in the last 10 years has made it incredibly easy for anyone, anywhere to publish a book. You can quickly create an Amazon KDP account, upload a document, use their cover design app and click Publish within 30 minutes.

But you shouldn't!

Being a self-published writer means taking care of your business. That's because you're really setting up a little publishing biz. And all the big details like editing, design and marketing have to be done by... you! Sure, you can ignore all that and put something quickly online but it won't sell. You're not going to build an audience without a plan. There is no magic shortcut. There is no app that will do it all for you.

At every stage of the book creation process, you need to be professional, measured and keeping an eye on the bigger strategy. If you aren't selling more books, then why are you even self-publishing? If it's just a hobby, there is nothing wrong with that. But remember, hobbies don't pay the rent. Treat your little publishing house like a business and it will reward you.

As far as your budget allows, enlist professional help to get your book to a stage where it's ready to be released to the world. It's an investment in your writing career - and your book deserves the best chance of success. If you self-publish a book, you are the publisher. So, to build your writer's 'brand' you need to take care of all of the details. It means the work doesn't stop at your first draft. It means hiring an editor and re-writing a second, third, fourth or even fifth draft. Whatever it takes to make your book as great as it can be. Don't rush. If you've got something to say to the world, do it properly or you're just wasting your time. Rushing is guaranteed to set you up for failure.

Self-publishing means hiring a layout artist so your book looks great and is easy to read. Remember, just because you can format a Microsoft Word document it doesn't mean you can format a book for print-on-demand or Kindle. There are design conventions for eBooks and print books that affect your book's quality and most importantly its readability. Hire in professional help. Your readers will thank you.

Being a self-published author also means you don't design your own book cover. There are some truly horrible self-created book covers out there. Don't be one of them! Book cover design is an art form. Invest in your product and hire a graphic designer (or use Canva).

Successful independent publishers take care of the details. That's because ignoring small details sets you up to fail. Small details like an unedited book with bad grammar or spelling. A sloppy or hard to read page layout. A truly awful, or at the very least bland, book cover. The lack of a strategy for selling your book. A non-existent or poorly executed writer's platform, distancing you from potential readers.

This is the truth about self-publishing. It's hard work.

If you're going to have any shot at building an audience and repeatedly selling books, you need to create the best possible version of your book. You have to be professional at every step of the book creation process. The whole point of building your writer's platform is to help sell your product - your book. If your product is sub-par, then building a platform is really not going to make any difference.

This book doesn't tell you how to write and prepare your book for self-publication. You may already be at that stage. This chapter aims to reinforce the importance of professionalism in what you are doing, because you'll need to bring that same attention to detail to your platform building efforts.

> TIP: *The real truth about self-publishing is you need to become much more than a writer. You need to become an authorpreneur.*

CHAPTER 5

The Rights and Wrongs of Self-Publishing

To build an effective writer's platform, you need to get comfortable using the tools and tricks of digital marketing. You have to become an authorpreneur (a blend of writer and owner of your very own little digital business).

To get started, all you need to spend is your time. The recent revolution in cloud computing means you no longer need to buy any software. You buy access to an app. Most of the apps mentioned in this book offer a free basic subscription. Some of the most powerful tools for self-publishing and marketing are available this way.

As your communication needs become more sophisticated (and I'll talk about that later), you can upgrade to more features when it makes business sense. By that point you would have established your little publishing empire and you'll be able to justify the cost. Even better, these costs are a legitimate tax deductible expense.

For now, the basic free versions of these apps offer all the tools you need to create the key elements of your writer's platform - website, mailing list, and a social media strategy to promote yourself and your writing.

Now, you may be thinking 'who has the time to do all this?' Think of it this way. Who is going to buy your book after your hard work creating it is done? If you don't have a marketing strategy, you'll just be spinning your wheels creating endless busy work.

At this point, there are really only two publishing methods open to you. I call them the 'hope' and platform publishing methods. Let's have a look.

Hope Publishing

'Hope' publishing is when you just throw something together and hope it will work. You write your book quickly, rush production (editing, layout and cover design) and eagerly upload it on KDP or Smashwords in the middle of the night. You have no strategy or plan apart from the hope that it does well.

Then what? Who is going to buy it? You sure hope someone does, but you need more than that to create success. When you 'hope' publish, you're lining up a whole lot of hopes. Who is going to KNOW about your book? Thousands of titles are self-published every day. You can buy ads on Google or Facebook and hope people will buy. You can hope that Amazon's algorithm might give your new book a little bump in the vast Amazonian self-published ocean. You hope it will not sink unnoticed. I've some bad news for you. 'Hope' publishing does not work. It never has. You need a writer's platform and a clear strategy.

Platform Publishing

Ok, let's look at the alternative scenario. You haven't left your success to hope. While you've been writing your book, you've also been slowly building your platform as part of a strategy to launch your book. You've realised that you can start building an audience before your book is even published.

The blog you started is gaining traction. You realised you only need to blog once a month, and focus on quality vs quantity. Your social media posts are engaging and on brand. Your social media publishing schedule is largely automated, but you take time to engage with people, offer advice, inject humour and personality, and grow your social media presence. Then, as your blog and social posts gain traction, you slowly start building a mailing list of fans. You've invested time building your free writer's platform, and know that you can easily maintain it for less than 30 minutes a day.

Finally you're ready to launch your book. Your hard work has paid off and you've built up a community of Twitter, Facebook and Instagram followers, and a mailing list of thousands of subscribers. As soon as you hit Publish, you send an email to your readers on your mailing list with a special offer for your new book. You drop a promotion link to your social media followers.

Now, what do think is going to happen? You won't 'hope' you'll sell books. You WILL sell books.

This is the key difference from 'hope' publishing. With your writer's platform, you'll sell books because you've engaged your followers with your pre-launch. You'll sell books because you have control of the most precious thing in marketing - a mailing list.

That is the power of the writer's platform. It exists to grow your mailing list of fans and readers. In this book, I'm going to look in detail at all the elements you need to build a successful platform and grow your mailing list using basic internet marketing techniques. I'm going to show you how to organise your time to manage all of this without impacting on your real work - writing.

You're going to learn that the two are not mutually exclusive. I'm going to show you how to build (and maintain) your writer's platform and still have time to write.

I'm going to show you how to take your first baby steps towards becoming an authorpreneur. I can't guarantee your success, but I can guarantee in that shouty writer's party your book will get the attention it deserves.

CHAPTER 6

Setting Your Self-Publishing Goals

Every business needs a strategy to survive. What you are creating - your little publishing business - is a business like any other. You need to know where you want it to go, and how you want it to grow.

These are important issues that require serious thought. There isn't an app that will do this for you. That's because if you don't have a clear plan of what you want to achieve with your writer's platform, you will fail. Without a clear strategy in place before you start building your platform, you'll just be wasting your time and effort.

Building a writer's platform must be driven by a strategy for finding and nurturing your readers. Now this is difficult when you first start, but you'll see it's not impossible. In the excitement of writing and self-publishing your book, it's easy to forget about your overall strategy.

It's understandable you just want to write your little book, quickly upload it to Kindle and count the money as it rolls into your bank account. You imagine Hollywood and Netflix producers, begging you for the movie rights to your heartbreaking work of staggering genius (with apologies to David Eggers).

Who wouldn't like a bit of that action? But, sadly, with very few exceptions, that will not happen. I tried that 'strategy' myself when I started and while it may give a few sales here and there, I'm here to tell you that does not a publishing career make.

Quickly rushing your book to market is not a strategy. So what is?

To develop your strategy, work backwards from your publishing goals. What do you want to achieve? Someone who self-publishes books on marketing with the intention of driving leads for a coaching program will have quite a different strategy from a young adult fiction author who intends to write and publish a new book every year.

In both of these examples you need to consider who is your market and where you are going to find them. How can you build rapport with them? How can you make them care enough about your book to buy it, and maybe buy another of yours?

Building your tribe is about connecting with people who will care enough to buy your book. It's about building an audience that may help you gain attention when you send query letters to publishers.

Your long term writing goals will help guide your strategy. Remember, you will use basic internet marketing techniques to grow and build your platform. And there is nothing set and forget about it. A successful internet marketer always analyses the market and changes their tactics when needed to suit their strategy.

Let's keep it simple. Your goal determines your strategy.

Don't overwhelm yourself with too many goals. You can do this by just visualising one big goal at a time. A good way to start mapping your writing and publishing goals is to brainstorm. Get some paper and a pen, and take 5 minutes to do some free association. Where do you want to be in 12 months time? What will your little writing and self-publishing business look like? What does success look like to you? Focus on this task without distractions and create a mind map of where you want to be.

Let's say your goal is to complete, publish and launch your first book in a series in 12 months' time and create an Amazon bestseller with 20 great reviews.

Now I'm deliberately omitting the 'writing the book' part. I'm assuming if you've come this far researching how to build your platform, it means you've already completed a couple of drafts and are close to publishing. Or maybe you've already self-published but want to do it better with your next book.

In this example, a 12 month timeframe is plenty of time to achieve your goal of building and growing your platform. Don't worry - you can do this without getting in the way of your actual writing. If you break your big goals down into achievable small tasks, you won't get overwhelmed.

This sounds simple, because it is - it's basic project management. The Sydney Opera House was built using the same approach, so it will work for your writing and self-publishing business.

> TIP: Remember, you need to adopt an attitude of BABY STEPS. Just do one thing at a time and you'll get there. Stay focused.

Fine Tuning Your Strategy

By now you've written down your goals in your brainstorming session. The strategy part is how you achieve those goals.

Let's look at our example goal again:

> *"To complete, publish and launch the first book in a series in 12 months' time and create an Amazon KDP bestseller with 10 great reviews"*

Now, your goal may be more modest, but let's tease out a 12 month strategy map:

- Build a website/blog and write about the things you love about your genre. Write about your book. Tease interest with sample chapters.
- Post on social media to raise awareness and drive traffic back to your blog.
- Capture email addresses from that traffic to start building a mailing list.
- Engage with your subscribers (in a non-spammy way) to get them to share your content.
- Build a list of 1000 subscribers pre-launch.
- Launch your book!
- Ask subscribers to submit reviews after your book launch.

- To have a platform and audience in place at the end of the 12 months that's positioned to grow and expand.

Now, that's a bare bones 12 month strategy that gives you a good idea WHY you're going to all this trouble to build a writer's platform. In the next section I'm going to look at the tactics behind achieving your strategy on each of these elements.

Tactics

Tactics are just the actual tasks you will do to follow your strategy and achieve your goals. You've mapped your goals and strategy for the next 12 months. Tactics are simply the HOW of getting there.

As I've said earlier in this book, building a writer's platform uses all of the basic tools of internet marketing. That is, a unified brand, a strong social media message, a mailing list and a strategy to build it. Building a writer's platform is internet marketing 101 and you should pay attention to the 'dark arts' employed to get you to download or buy something, because they are GREAT for building platforms and selling books too!

Building your writer's platform is part of your marketing campaign to sell books. The elements of your platform are the tactics you'll employ to implement your strategy to achieve your goal.

CHAPTER 7

Making It All Happen

In the last chapter I talked about how to reach your goal with the right strategy and tactics; not just creating endless work for yourself. You may think PM (project management) is all about building big things, but the truth is PM techniques are just as useful for IP (intellectual property) projects - like yours!

What happens in PM is you define your big goals (milestones), and list the tasks you need to complete to hit your milestones. It's an easy way to keep track of a project and see at a glance what needs to be done. It's like a giant to-do list. Importantly, some milestones are dependent on other tasks (and milestones) being completed. Identify these 'critical tasks' so you carry out your tactics in the right order.

Now, this isn't a book about project management. There are many that can give you a deeper dive if you're interested. The basic techniques though, are just as useful for building a house, making a movie or publishing a book. There are pathways that are followed for any similar project. So, once you get your project organised, you'll find you can duplicate the process over and over again.

PM techniques keep you on track, keep you in control of your project, stop you procrastinating and prevent you missing critical steps.

There are some powerful software applications used for PM (for example, Microsoft Project), but you don't need this. PM can be done with a notepad and some post-it notes. The key to good PM techniques is planning, review, execution and post-project review. Let's briefly look at all four.

Planning

You have to map out every single task and sub-task of your publishing project. For platform development, it's best to think of a 12 month plan that finishes with the launch of your book. As you plan your big goal (developing your platform and launching your book) you'll quickly see that each component can have its own sub-projects. Each sub-project also has its own milestones.

By putting the time into planning, you'll create a solid PM plan for your project. The trick to efficient PM planning is identifying the milestones and giving them a MBFB date (Must Be Finished By). This way, you can quickly see what is urgent and non-urgent, and focus on urgent tasks to be much more efficient with the little time you have.

A quick way to project plan is just stick some post-it notes on a wall. This gives you a visual overview of the whole project. You can see what's needed, move tasks around and it costs practically nothing.

Once you have mapped out your launch plan, I recommend putting the milestone dates into a calendar. It can be electronic or on paper, although I do prefer using a wall chart, as you can see your entire project at a glance. Even better, you get the satisfaction of crossing off the days and tasks as you near completion.

Review

All failed projects have one thing in common (by failed I mean over budget, incomplete or not fit for purpose). That one thing is failure to review. Once you have planned and commenced the project, you have to review your status every week. Line by line. You have to know if you're about to miss a looming milestone. If you do, the domino effect in your carefully constructed project can result in chaos.

The review process can take less than one hour each week. Just check how everything is travelling and if any tasks needs to be re-prioritised. You'll find as you review, priorities do change as your milestones get closer. The key is to be flexible. Regular review is just as important as your initial project planning. Probably even more so.

Execution

This is where the rubber hits the road on any project. A plan is just a plan. It's how that plan is executed that determines success or failure of your project. You want to execute each element of your project plan to the best of your ability. What you can't do is waste time by backtracking and redoing tasks a second or third time. The execution mantra is simply this - do it once and do it well.

You may outsource some elements of your publishing and platform building project. If you do, it's your job as project manager to make sure they complete that work to your standard.

When every element of a project plan is executed accurately and on time, you'll see your milestones stay in place and your project will stay within budget. In this case, I'm trying to help you do as much as possible, for as low a cost as possible.

Post-Project Review

If you are going to publish more than one book, post-project review is another essential phase of PM. No project runs perfectly. It's always useful to learn what went wrong, what went well, and what could have been done even better.

By understanding this, you'll be able to improve how you run your next project. In your case, your next book launch. Serial project management is a learning environment. Make each one better and don't repeat mistakes. The post mortem is how you do this.

> TIP: At the end of the book there is a link to a PM planning resource template you can download.

So, as I hope you can see, project management is how you get your shit done. Now, let's start at the beginning. To embark on your platform building and writing project you need the right tools.

CHAPTER 8

The Power of Blogging

An effective writer's platform uses many of the tools in the internet marketer's toolbox. Content marketing is a powerful way to establish your credentials, create regular online content and grow your mailing list. Your blog is how you do this - it's the central plank of your writer's platform. There are some great reasons to get excited about blogging.

Blogging is a Regular Writing Practice

If you're just starting out and are struggling with motivation, you'll discover blogging is a great cure for writer's block. That's because deadlines do work. Blogging is a great way to practice your writing while committing to a public deadline. It's one thing working in isolation on your book that nobody but you will read in the short term. Quite another to commit to a regular publishing schedule.

Remember, you only need to post once a month. The key is quality over quantity. Consider your target audience. What would they like to read about? If you define this early on, you can keep a list of blog ideas, giving you a 'supply chain' from idea to draft to published post. In this way, 750 words a month are not hard to manage.

Blogging Improves Your Writer's Website SEO

By now you know the reason to build a writer's website is to grow a mailing list of potential readers. To entice readers to sign up you need a steady stream of traffic. You can pay for ads on Facebook, Twitter or

Google, but it's much easier (and free) to make sure your blog posts follow basic SEO practices. Search Engine Optimisation is a huge topic, but to get you started I've added some resources in the Free Tools chapter at the back of the book.

Good SEO means that your website appears at the top of Google searches, so you'll get free traffic. Some of that traffic will sign up to your offer. Some will check out your social profiles. Some may even buy your book. Google loves websites that regularly update content, so one blog post a month will push your website up the rankings.

Blogging Connects You With Future Readers

When you start out, no-one knows who you are. Blogging allows you to define your unique writer's personality to your future readers.

You've gone to all this trouble to build a writer's platform. If you want readers to be interested in what you have to say and maybe hang around until you actually publish your book, you have to entertain. The trick is finding a balance to staying on brand about your writing while also revealing a little of yourself.

It sounds overwhelming but you can manage it. The trick is scheduling, which I'll cover in the next chapter. Basically, it's deciding how often you want to blog, and following a schedule to do it.

Most bloggers start out with the idea of blogging once a week. So they begin with a lot of enthusiasm but after a month or so they run out of ideas and the blog slowly disappears.

Here's how to prevent it. To start with, one blog post a month is plenty. Keep it to about 750 words (which is a good length for Google and SEO). The hardest thing about blogging is coming up with topics to blog about. You're a writer, after all, so the actual content shouldn't be a problem. If you're going to blog once a month, you only need a rolling list of 12 topics. This way, you'll never be pressed for an idea.

Each month brainstorm 12 ideas. As you go on, you'll find some new ideas are better than older ones. It's all good. Work on the better idea.

I use the Evernote (www.evernote.com) and Drafts (https://getdrafts.com) apps on my phone. That way whenever a blog topic pops into my head I can easily capture it. Use what you like - pen and paper, Google Docs, whatever works for you. The object is to capture ideas and use them!

Schedule your blog writing time. Once you have a moveable feast of blog topics to select from, you need to schedule writing time to knock those 750 words into shape. Begin by scheduling 30 minutes at the start of each month to do the following:

- review your topics
- choose the monthly blog topic
- write the content.

Now the last part may sound scary if you're juggling a job or family commitments, but let me share a simple hack for producing regular blog content:

- set a regular blog publish date in your calendar
- work backwards.

Let's look at that in detail. Four weeks from the publish date your project should look like this:

- Week 1: begin first draft
- Week 2: complete and edit first draft
- Week 3: complete and edit second draft
- Week 4: publish

Let's look deeper...

Week 1: Begin first draft

I'm not talking War and Peace here. Just a 750 word blog. If you're keeping a list of topics, once you choose one you can throw down 750-1000 words in your first draft. Remember that NO ONE IS GOING TO SEE YOUR FIRST DRAFT EXCEPT YOU.

Just pump it out, typos and all. The purpose of a first draft is to dump what's in your brain onto the screen. Once it's there you can start polishing and editing. Week 1 is just committing to your topic and writing about it. You shouldn't need to spend longer than 30 minutes on this. Then put it away for the weekend and stop thinking about it.

Week 2: Complete and edit first draft

The best self-editing method is simply printing out your work and reviewing it with a red pen. This changes the context. Once you see those words off screen and on a page you'll easily see the flaws in your writing. Try reading passages aloud. Here's a tip: if it sounds clunky when you read it that's because it is. Get that red pen and be ruthless. Slash, burn, make comments. Draw arrows where you're going to rearrange sentences and paragraphs or drop them entirely.

Have fun. Kill your darlings.

Now put that first draft aside. That's all you need to do for week 2.

Week 3: Complete and edit second draft

A week later, type up your editing suggestions from last week's session. As you edit, you'll find the prose comes alive as you slice and dice hyperbole, repetition and padding. By the end of week 3 you'll have your final draft ready for publication.

Week 4: Publish

You have a monthly publishing deadline, and if you use this method you will have content you'll be proud to publish each month. Use your last 30 minutes to load the copy, check SEO and, finally, publish.

Now you've published, just start over again. Brainstorm and review blog topics, then begin at Week 1 for next month's blog post.

Here's a great example of a freeform writer's blog from John Birmingham (https://cheeseburgergothic.substack.com/).

CHAPTER 9

Getting Social

Having a blog is just one part of the platform puzzle, but it's not enough by itself. In this chapter I'm going to talk about some online marketing tactics that work as well for authors as any other online business.

First, let's talk about brand building. Because that's what you're building here. The end game is your very own online business identity that is a self-sustaining way to generate cash flow by selling books.

I know some of you will recoil from this. You'll be wondering how the hell can I waste time on all this platform building when I really want to sit in my room and write my perfect books that everyone will love.

Well, good luck with that because becoming a self-published writer takes a bit of work and a carefully planned strategy. How you organise your time and approach the whole project of platform building will be key to your success.

Social media is crucial to building your readership. You need to engage your brand - YOU the writer - across all the social platforms. It's quite possible to do this without being pushy, needy or a downright pain in the rear. BUT do it you must.

Think of your platform like a wheel (I know, I'm mixing metaphors again but stick with me). The hub of the wheel, around which everything spins, is your blog and mailing list. The spokes in the wheel are Twitter, Facebook, Pinterest and Instagram. You can use some or all of these. I'd recommend doing some research to find where your audience hangs out. For example, young adult fiction readers might be better reached through Instagram. Other genres may work better with

Facebook. Every social media site will generate different types of traffic back to your blog (and mailing list). This is why it's essential to cultivate ALL social platforms as lead channels for your platform.

Strategy

Before raising a finger, you must decide on your strategy. Otherwise you'll just be making endless work for yourself that will get in the way of your actual writing. Remember, the purpose of building a platform is to build a readership and audience, and you need a strategy for how you go about doing that. Every post you put out on social media must align with your brand, be correctly #hashtagged and have a CTA (call to action). That's because the only reason to post to social media is to engage your audience and hopefully push that engagement back to your writer's website to help grow your mailing list.

Let's look at them all in turn.

Branding

Good brands have consistency across platforms. Everything aligns - colours, fonts, graphics, logo. (A word on logos - don't get hung up on them. You're not Apple or Coca Cola, you're a writer. Don't waste money or time on a logo at this stage). Emulating standard marketing branding practices makes you look more professional.

You should strive for a consistent look and feel on your writer's website and social media accounts. Basically, everywhere a potential reader interacts with you, they'll see they are in the same 'ecosystem'.

Most importantly, it's about trust. If you gain a reader's trust in one medium (say Twitter) and you invite them to join your website's mailing list, they'll know they're in the right place if your branding aligns. They'll transfer their trust. And the opposite is also true.

You don't have to spend a fortune on your brand. Just be consistent with your look, your graphics, your #hashtags and most importantly what you write about and share with your readers. Remember that every person who decides to follow you does so for a reason. They find you entertaining, or like the information you share. If you suddenly veer off script, you'll break that trust and lose a follower.

Every follower you gather on social media is a potential reader on your platform's mailing list. You have to treat this relationship with the utmost respect.

Branding can get quite deep, and if you want to take a deep dive into it I recommend 30 Day Marketing Challenge by Rachel at Bad Redhead Media as a starting point (you'll find a link at the end of this book).

Let's use a romance fiction writer as an example. Everything a romance writer blogs and all social media engagement should be consistent with the romance genre. From the font you use in your blog, to your header art, to the colours you use. This includes the selection of blog topics to write about. The channels you interact with on Twitter, Facebook, Instagram and Pinterest. The #hashtags you use are crucial. You also have to decide whether you're trying to attract readers or writers, or a combination of both.

Hashtags

Hashtags are a powerful way for readers to find you. They are the #symbols that appear as words during a post, or in a list at the end. They are very useful for tying your post to other similar posts, by flagging areas of interest. They are a channel marker in the endless (and bottomless) internet river. Used correctly, hashtags are a very powerful way to amplify your social posts to a much wider audience.

For example, popular hashtags for writers on Twitter are #amwriting and #writingcommunity. If you use these tags, everyone in those communities can see your post, and like, comment or share it. You might want to tag #amwritingromance. You get the drift.

A word of warning. If you just follow and interact with other writers (which is great) don't be surprised when your Twitter feed is filled with 'BUY MY BOOK' tweets. Interacting with fellow writers is amazing, and a great way to boost confidence and engage in discussions about writing. But you need to also target the audiences you're after, so do a bit of research.

> *TIP: Just type # and experiment with variations to see what comes up. For example #amreading might suggest #amreadingromance or*

#amreadingscifi. Look in the Free Tools chapter to find a list of useful hashtags for Twitter, Facebook and Instagram.

CTA (Call to Action)

I know, more dreaded internet marketing speak to rob you of your precious writing time. CTAs are quite simple - it's just asking the reader to do what you want. Here's an example: an ad for a holiday has at the bottom in large print: CALL 1800 000 000 to book your place.

Marketing is useless without ASKING the reader to do what you want them to. It's no good asking at the top of the page or the middle. A good CTA is the last thing they'll read on your page, ad or social post.

Again, this isn't a book about internet marketing. In the Free Tools chapter, I've listed a few free resources to help you crafting CTAs.

Now, a big caveat. DON'T jump into Twitter saying BUY MY BOOK, BUY MY BOOK BUY MY BOOK. Because no-one will. What you want is for people to discover your blog and possibly join your mailing list. So your CTA should simply point people to your blog.

Of course, this all changes when you DO have a book to promote and sell. The CTA should be a link to where people can actually buy your book. Ideally, you'll have a page set up on your writer's website where people can easily buy your book. More about this later.

Twitter

Twitter is a great way to build your brand and gain followers. A quick ways to do this is by engaging with writing communities and sharing a bit of love. Use the #writingcommunity and #readingcommunity hashtags and join in the conversations. You'll find an incredible group of supportive writers and readers. You can ask questions, and find other writers who are working in your genre. But don't push all your marketing to #writingcommunity. While it's a great place to connect with writers, remember your marketing should be targeted at readers.

Design an eye-catching Twitter header graphic. Do it yourself using Canva (canva.com). They have templates ready to go in the right size for every social channel: Twitter, Facebook, Instagram. So you can create a design and just resize it for reuse on another platform. If your design skills are not up to scratch you can hire someone on Fiverr (fiverr.com) for a few bucks. (Fiverr is a great way to inexpensively source anyone to do anything, including graphic design).

Remember to keep your branding consistent. If you already have a book to sell, make sure it is featured in your header art. Also make it easy for people to find out more about your book (and buy it) by adding links to your book's and writer's website.

Facebook

Don't use your private Facebook account for your writer's platform. Create a separate writer's page. Once again make sure your branding is consistent. Make sure you create a great banner image for your page (that's the one that splashes across the top). Again, be consistent with your branding. Use Canva to design your graphics.

A great Facebook feature is 'Notes'. Think of it like a magazine page. Splash a big header image at the top, a headline, and have complete control over the layout with a CTA at the end (it can even be BUY MY BOOK!). You can create an About page using Notes. It looks classy, and lets you provide info about you and set the tone of your page.

> TIP: Research where your readers interact online. Facebook now serves a much older demographic. Is your audience there? You may not need it.

Instagram

Instagram is a great platform for sharing a bit about your life and yourself. The same rules apply as before. Don't use your personal Instagram account. Create a new one for your writer 'persona'. Think about what you're going to post about. The key with Instagram is that it's an image-based medium. Some writers use Instagram very effectively to post about travel and their WIPS (works in progress).

Where Instagram works best is if you use it to let readers peek behind the curtain of your writer's life. One of the most effective users of Instagram I've seen is science fiction writer Gareth Powell. He uses Instagram to talk about his life, show what he's doing, what he's working on, food and drink, and travel. Importantly, he keeps it in the

SF realm, so he never wanders off-brand. All with a bit of wit and warmth. Instagram works well when you are sharing images from your work and life. Again, hashtagging is key to expanding your audience (there's a hashtag guide in Free Tools to get you started).

> TIP: Don't forget to use your branding, with the header image, author bio and links back to your writer's website, books and other social accounts.

Trolls

I've left this till last, because unfortunately there are people who like to stir up controversy on social media. They can be boorish, rude, racist, misogynistic and worse. They hide behind fake IDs and photos. Welcome to the world of the troll. It's likely that you will, at some point, be trolled. The best advice is simply Don't Feed The Trolls.

If you do get a negative comment - or worse - don't take it personally. Trolls thrive on confrontation and it's a fight you can never win. The simplest thing is to just ignore them. Block them. If they are really vile, report them as well. Personally, I've never had many problems. I follow my own advice and just block anyone that is being downright rude. What do you do if you are the victim of what's called 'shitposting' and tagging about your own work? Unfortunately nothing. If you are using social media to promote your brand, you have to prepare yourself for the eventuality of being trolled. It's all in how YOU respond. If you are honest in your work and promotions you shouldn't have any problems.

CHAPTER 10

Using Podcasts to Promote Your Book

Podcasts are a great way of promoting your book and platform. Do some research and find the podcasts that best align with your brand and what you're trying to achieve. Appearing on a podcast should be a part of your book marketing strategy.

While it's best to leave this to your book launch promotion phase, it doesn't hurt to start researching now and compiling a list of podcasts you could be interviewed on.

I have run a podcast called 'EBR - The Writers' Show' for quite a while, and have learned a bit about what makes good 'talent' (what makes a good guest and what makes a bad guest).

Why be on a Podcast?

It's all about reaching a wider audience and driving traffic back to your writer's platform and ultimately selling books. The mathematics are pretty simple. Podcasters are always looking for guests. If you approach a podcaster respectfully and ask for a spot, you'll often get one. When you approach them, don't waste their time or yours so be prepared, polite and straight to the point.

Be ready for knock-backs and don't give up. When you do get on a show, be respectful, be good talent, know your subject and keep it short. The best podcast interviews are generally about 30 minutes. You can easily do this if you stick to this guide.

How to Approach Podcasters

The easiest way to approach podcasters is through email. A word of warning: don't ever direct message them on Twitter! A lot of people don't like being approached this way. Most podcasts have an associated website where each episode is posted with show notes. You'll be able to find a contact form or email address there.

Create a spreadsheet to keep track of your approaches:

SHOW NAME | HOST NAME | PODCAST URL | CONTACT DATE | FOLLOW UP DATE | INTERVIEW? (Y/N) | INTERVIEW DATE

It's important to do your research before you approach podcasters. After you shortlist the podcasts you think would be a good fit for your brand and book, listen to a few episodes to make sure. Use Stitcher (stitcher.com) to search for your shortlisted podcasts and listen without having to download any apps.

Keep your email short and to the point. People are time poor. If you get right to the point you'll have a much better chance of becoming a guest. Make sure to keep a copy of your email.

To help put your email together, use this template:

> Dear [hostname],
>
> I love your podcast [name of show], and would like to be a guest if you have time to fit me in. I'm about to launch my new book [book name] which is about [quick synopsis].
>
> I listened to [research episode name that fits] and immediately thought I'd be a good fit for your show.
>
> Here's my website and book [link to your platform].
>
> Look forward to hearing from you.
>
> Regards
>
> [your name]
>
> www.yourwritersplatform.com

That's it. Simple isn't it? Polite and to the point. You wait for a follow up (this is why you need to log your approaches in a spreadsheet). Follow up in a month. If you get a definite yes/no response, update your spreadsheet. You can follow up once more after that, but if you still don't receive a reply, just move on to the next in the list.

Most podcasters will send you a calendar link so you can set the date and time. Some will ask for a list of questions you'd like to be asked.

How to Pivot to Your CTA

This gets back to your platform. You want to talk about your book, how you wrote it - and a bit about you. But at the end of the interview, you need to plug your book and your CTA. Just be straightforward. Usually the interviewer will indicate they're wrapping up. This is your cue to finish with something like:

'Thanks for having me on the show. Anybody that would like to find out more about my book and what I'm writing, just go to [your platform URL].'

Most podcasters are happy to add this info themselves, but never assume it. Sometimes they just forget to ask, and end the interview. At that point it's too late and your interview will be broadcast without a CTA. It's not the end of the world, but it's not ideal as you've wasted an opportunity to promote your book and platform.

How to Wrap it up with the Podcaster

After the interview has finished, you'll stay on the line for a few minutes. Make sure you thank the podcaster for their time and tell them you'll send them the links for your platform and book.

DON'T FORGET THIS. Follow up immediately.

Podcasters are time poor and may not have the time to search the web for your stuff to add to their show notes. They'll be grateful and most will include your info in the show notes.

This is important, because some podcasts have great reach. This is why you need to talk about your platform on the podcast and also have it included on their show notes.

Don't forget to promote your podcast appearance on your own platform. Blog about it. Boost it on Facebook and Twitter. Email your list. Let everyone know about it and provide links to the episode.

That's it! Good luck! Podcasts are a fantastic way to drive traffic back to your mailing list, but ONLY if you're on the right podcast. Do your research first.

> *TIP: If you're writing a romance novel, research podcasts that talk about romantic fiction. It's as basic as that. Don't waste time on podcasts where your potential readers will not be.*

If you appear on a podcast with a reach of 10,000 listeners per month and only 5% of them are interested enough to visit your website and buy your book, that's 500 sales you didn't have before.

CHAPTER 11

Building Your Writer's Blog and Website

Let's talk about your writer's website and blog! The blog is the hub of your writer's platform. The best way to create a blog for free is using Wordpress (WP), the king of blog platforms. It's 100% free and easy to use. If you can write an email, you can use Wordpress. You can create a great writer's website using its free templates. Remember, the aim of this book is to help you get your platform rolling without unnecessary cost.

Why Are There Two Wordpresses?

There are two versions of Wordpress - even though it's actually the same Wordpress. But it's not so confusing. On the free wordpress.com you just create an account and start blogging immediately.

Then there is wordpress.org. This is the same Wordpress software, but the core Wordpress engine is available for download if you want to install and run Wordpress on your own server. This gives you more control over the look and feel and performance of your website and blog. Some businesses do this: for example, Siteground, Godaddy and Bluehost charge you monthly hosting fee for a business-grade Wordpress installation. You can also have your own domain name (www.myauthorname.com) which you can't do in the free version. There are great reasons to do that, but right now, you don't need to. This is about building your writing platform on the cheap - and wordpress.com is the way to do it.

Let's get started:

1. Create an account

Easy - just visit <u>wordpress.com</u> and create an account. Once you log in to your account you can start creating your site.

Domain name vs sub-domain name? Let's pick that apart - this is geek talk after all. A domain name is simply wordpress.com or if you want to get fancy yourname.com.

A sub-domain is yourname.wordpress.com. I recommend this because it's free. If you want to get fancy with your own domain, you'll have to pay Wordpress a small monthly hosting fee - which at time of writing starts about $10 per month. But I want to keep this new platform of yours completely free - so we'll stick with the sub-domain for now.

Remember you can upgrade to a domain name anytime later if you want to. You should give some thought to what this would be. That's because there's a lot of work in front setting up the rest of your platform and it's much easier to get the name right now, than to change it further down the track.

When selecting a sub-domain or a domain name, there is one thing to consider. Your platform is about you as an author, so you should use your author's name (either your real name or a nom de plume). Don't name your platform after your book - once you move onto your next project, your website will be redundant.

> *TIP: When you set up your free account you may find that the name you want is already taken. This is bad news for John Smith. If you have an unusual name, you may be lucky. Instead, think of an unusual handle. For example, if John Doe is a SF writer maybe johndoescifiwriter would work. You get the picture - get creative. Don't settle for johndoe387.*

Finally, I do recommend buying your domain name (even just to sit on it). Domains only cost $12 a year. Better to buy it it now and use it later than to find out someone has bought it when you do need it.

2. Pick your theme

Wordpress allows you to change the look and the feel of your website by selecting a theme. The free version allows you some limited customisation. It's a matter of taste but just pick what you fancy. A WP theme is like redecorating your home. There's some great free themes available. Remember, your author's website is the core part of your writer's platform, so you want your brand look and feel to lock into all your social media channels.

3. Create the pages

Ok, you've got the basic tech stuff set up. And remember - the website is not published until you're ready to do so. I advise not to publish until you have at least one blog post ready to go.

Let's have a look at some standard pages you can create:

About the Author

It's a bit embarrassing writing about yourself. My advice is to just stand back and see yourself through a reader's eyes. There's no need to go into great detail - just a bit about why you write, what you've written, and a glimpse into the real you. That said, there is a difference between non-fiction and fiction authors' 'About' pages. With non-fiction, it's important to focus on who you are. People want to know about your background and expertise. Why should they listen to you? With fiction, if you're just starting out you can be a bit more freewheeling about yourself.

I recommend looking at other authors' 'About' pages to get a sense of it. Here's some great examples:

JF Penn https://jfpenn.com

Hugh Howey https://hughhowey.com/about/

This profile on Reedsy has great advice:

https://blog.reedsy.com/about-the-author-examples/

Contact Page

Use a standard contact form, as included in all Wordpress templates. Don't put a clickable email address on a webpage - it will be harvested by spam bots and you'll start receiving all kinds of spam email. The contact form hides your email address under a layer of web wizardry so it is much safer. I don't recommend putting a phone number on your page at all (unless you are actually running a business).

Mailing List Registration Form

Remember the main reason for building a writer's platform is to grow your mailing list. I'll talk about this in more detail in the next chapter. Right now, you just need to consider where the form is going to go. You usually put the mailing list form in three places on your website:

- As a banner across the top of the page
- On the side bar (if your page has one)
- At the end of each blog post.

It should have a solid CTA (Call to Action). Why should people give you their email address? It could be to get more blog posts sent to their inbox. Maybe you want to put a newsletter together featuring free chapters of your book or talking about your writing process. Maybe you could get really creative and write a helpful little pdf book on a topic close to your heart that you give away for a free download.

There's many ways to craft a CTA (and what happens after). In the Marketing Resources chapter, I list some great sources that delve deeper into this topic.

When to Publish?

Not until you're ready is the answer. It's important to make sure everything is in order. A quick release checklist for a website is:

- Do all the page links work?
- Is the writing tight?
- No grammar or spelling or typo issues?
- Are the images you are using optimised for the web?

The easiest way to lose visitors is having very large images on your website that are not optimised - your pages will take a long time to load and in this impatient world, no-one will wait more than a few seconds. Check out Free Tools at the end of this book for more info.

Make sure that your social media cross-links all work: Twitter, Facebook, Instagram, LinkedIn.

While you should take great care in setting everything up, don't forget that once you publish you can change and tweak to your heart's content. Use the 90/10 rule. You'll find that your website/blog will be largely complete for all purposes at 90%. The additional 10% of tweaking will take up just as much time as the initial 90%, so it's best to launch at 90% and start tweaking.

> TIP: Remember that a blog is a work in progress, but you should take care that your 'first edition' is as good as you can make it.

What to do After You Publish

Once you publish, you need to keep creating new content. Set up a blogging schedule and stick to it. There's really no need to blog more than once a month. Most new bloggers try to blog too often and quickly run out of things to say - as well as getting quite exhausted. If you stick to a monthly schedule and make sure you have a process to harvest ideas and move drafts along your 'pipeline', you'll be fine.

To track my blog pipeline I use Google Sheets (check out my free template download in the Free Tools chapter at the end of the book).

Finally, if you've enabled comments on your blog, remember to engage with readers who do leave a comment. I recommend installing Google Analytics to track your visitors.

A website/blog is a live document and in some ways it's never finished. The upside is you can always tweak and perfect it.

CHAPTER 12

Why You Need to Grow a Mailing List

The heart of any online marketing campaign is the mailing list. There's an old saying in marketing that "the money is in the list". This is as true for authors building a platform as it is for anyone trying to sell anything online.

Now, stick with me. I know some of you are no doubt turned off about talk of internet marketing but, as I've said many times, building a writer's platform is all about building your brand. And being able to reach out to your readers is the best way to build that brand.

> TIP: The mailing list is the most powerful way to build a relationship with your buyers. Even better, no-one can take that list of readers away from you.

It doesn't matter how many followers you have on Facebook, Instagram or Twitter because you don't really own the audience or the platform. If Twitter changes its rules, algorithm or simply closes down (however unlikely), all your followers will disappear overnight.

You are at the mercy of the algorithms wielded by these tech giants. When you post content, there is no guarantee all your followers will see your posts. The algorithms will only show your posts to those who regularly read or interact with you. So, you could have thousands of followers on Facebook but only get seen by a tiny fraction. The giants make sure the only way ALL your followers will get your message is if you pay for targeted advertising. That's how they make their money.

How about a system where you can contact ALL of your subscribers ALL of the time and it doesn't cost you anything? That is the power of direct email. You own it. You can talk directly to your audience whenever you want. No algorithm is going to determine who sees your message. It's simple as sending an email.

So, growing your mailing list is an incredibly important platform strategy. Probably THE most important.

You may have a pretty Facebook page with thousands of 'likes'. You may have many more people following you on Twitter or Instagram - but nothing works better than direct email contact if done correctly. Likes are a dime a dozen and at the end of the day don't really mean anything. It's easy to half read something on social media and 'like it' and move on. But if someone has taken the trouble to actually sign up for your mailing list, they're already pre-qualified for your message.

A pre-qualified lead is more likely to read your content and share it. They are more likely to consider your offer and even buy it. If you've carefully cultivated your writer's brand, the people on your email list will be your tribe. They'll be interested in what you have to say. Keep them engaged with timely useful content. Build their trust. Then you'll have a list that may actually buy your book when it's released.

That said, with great power comes great responsibility. If you build a mailing list DON'T SPAM YOUR PEOPLE. That's because people can just as easily unsubscribe from your list if you don't deliver what they want. Don't be sleazy. Don't be 'buy my book buy my book buy my book'. Give real value and you'll generate real loyalty.

How to Build a List

As I've already touched on, the mailing list is a simple, effective tool for the digital marketer (that's you). I've listed some excellent list building resources in Free Tools at the end of the book. The go-to resource for internet marketing advice is Hubspot.

List building is a huge topic, but I'll give you some simple advice to get started. The key part of a mailing list is the registration form on your website, and the 'what happens next' when someone subscribes to your list. The first two elements are the form and response.

Let's look at the form. You need to give people a reason to fill out the form to join your mailing list. It sounds simple but is also difficult. Why should people give you (or any marketer) their email address?

The answer is something called the CTA (Call to Action). A good CTA will offer something useful (and free), and be easy for the subscriber to use (no friction). Friction means anything on the form that makes it harder for the user to make a snap decision about joining.

Imagine two forms. One just asks for a first name and email address. The other asks for an email address, first name, last name and telephone number. The second form has more 'friction'. Unless you are actually making a sale, all you need to communicate with people on your list is an email address and their first name.

So, you've designed a frictionless form. What then? People won't give you their email address without a reason. You probably hate spam as much as I do. The only reason people will trust you with their email address is if your offer (your CTA) resonates and fills a need.

Let's look at some examples of simple CTAs (a reminder this is not a pro lesson on internet list building. I'll defer to Hubspot for that).

If you've been growing your writer's platform, and sharing your blog posts, you might have a simple CTA like "Join my mailing list and don't miss out on a blog post in the future". That's pretty basic and might elicit a 'so-what' from most people.

Imagine you said 'Join my private club and get my blog updates and pre-release chapters from my next book'. If you're engaging well with your followers on social media, this works much better.

Finally, if you have already published something that you'd like to give away (this is a common tactic with authors who have self-published a few books), use 'Join my list and get a free copy of my book'.

There are many ways to craft a good mailing list CTA. What they have in common is an understanding of the people who should be on the list. To be an effective internet marketer you need to understand your 'avatar'. An avatar is shorthand for the type of person likely to be in your audience. Let's say you write young adult vampire fiction. Your avatar may be young men and women aged 14 to 28, with an interest in vampires, romance etc.

Understanding your avatar will help guide you with content creation and list building. Curate your mailing list by deep avatar research. Let that research determine everything from the design of your forms to the content they'll receive from you. If you've carefully cultivated your avatars and have the right people on your list, when the time comes they may even buy your book.

Auto-Responders

This is the 'what happens next' after someone fills out the form on your writer's website. An auto-responder sends an automated email to everyone who subscribes to your list. This is an important email to craft because it's the first one they'll receive from you. A good auto-responder message will have a simple welcome, and a bit about what to expect next. Again, there are many detailed online resources about email copywriting (check out the Free Tools chapter). My tip is don't be corporate. Be yourself. Have a bit of fun, but stay on brand. Remember, if someone is reading your blog and follows up on your CTA, it's because they like your voice and trust you. So, whatever voice you've developed in your blog, keep it going.

Here's an example from my own writer's blog:

> SUBJECT: Hi, [first name]. You are my new favourite! 😀
>
> Hello [first name],
>
> Thanks for joining my little club. Because you're my new favourite, I'm going to give you a free copy of my first book 'Beautiful Lies'.
>
> People that are not my fav have to pay a few bucks. Just click here, or on the cover below!
>
> What else to expect? Well, from time to time I'll share some more exclusive short stories and behind the scenes fuss of this writing biz that won't be on the blog.
>
> I'll also let you know when I've got a new blog update that you might find amusing.
>
> Most of all, I'm going to keep you up to date about my new book, called 'The Watchers', which you'll be first to see.

So, thanks for joining my little club. Hope you enjoy the book. There's some SF stories, some of unbearable sadness, a couple of laughs and an enigmatic ending.

I'd be royally chuffed if you could give me a review as well.

Oh, and this is a real email address. I'm me. I'm not a Borg. If you write to me, I'll write back.

Talk soon
Geoff H

PS: What I WON'T do is spam you with nonsense. Promise.

That's it. A bit of exclusivity. A free gift. A promise of what's to come and a promise not to spam. Now, anyone reading my blog would recognise the same voice. This is important in any digital marketing. The fancy word for it is 'congruence'. Every element of your digital marketing strategy must 'follow' from the last step your customer took. In my example, the voice follows through but your design elements must align as well. Simply put, just ensure colours and fonts are the same at each customer touch point. It reassures the customer that they are following the correct path. Make sense?

Digital marketing is a huge subject. Hubspot (hubspot.com) and Copyblogger (copyblogger.com) have fantastic free resources if you want to deep dive into the ever evolving world of digital marketing.

Doing it Simply

This sounds quite complex and expensive, but there is a free entry-level email management platform - Mailchimp (mailchimp.com).

There are many far more sophisticated mail platforms, but they also cost $$$ per month. Digital marketing professionals use email platforms like Hubspot, Active Campaign and Infusion Soft. They all have free trial plans (usually first month free) but Mailchimp is the only platform with an actual free plan. It's based on the number of subscribers - free up to 1,000, once you hit that milestone it only costs a cup of coffee per month to go up a tier, unlocking more features.

The free Mailchimp plan doesn't have the sophisticated automation of the other platforms, but you don't need that at this early stage. As your writer's platform grows, and you begin selling books, you may justify the expense, but right now the free plan will do just fine.

Mailchimp's free version will let you create a simple form and embed it in your Wordpress site (we'll get to that later). It allows you to set up a simple auto-responder. You can design snazzy looking emails to send out to your mailing list. Perfect!

Your auto-responder email is just the start of your relationship with your mailing list. As your list grows, you'll be mailing directly to your list. Which begs the question… what to mail to your list?

What to Mail

My advice is to start simple. The first thing to mail out is alerts about new blog posts - summarise it in an email and send it to your subscribers. Ask them to share it, so you get more subscribers and more shares and… well, you get the picture. Most people who subscribed to your list probably wanted blog updates.

As your list grows, you'll find it's a great way to engage directly with your readers. If your new book is at a stage where you need beta readers, just hop on Mailchimp and ask your mailing list. At launch time, you could offer discounts to your list in exchange for reviews.

If you want to monetise your list, you could find some affiliate products that align with your brand and offer them (in a non-sleazy way) to your list - thus earning a percentage profit (see the section on affiliate marketing in the Marketing Resources chapter).

You can ask your list for feedback on cover design, titles, excerpts from your book. You can publicise in-store appearances. You can publish your book launch directly to your list. If you have built a list of a few hundred followers, what a great way to get some momentum for your book. Remember, your subscribers are following YOU because they are interested in your books and writing.

There are many options for a savvy email marketer. You'll find the successful ones follow the main rule of list building and client communication which is DON'T BE SLEAZY. Never forget, you've been trusted with an email address. In this age, that's a big deal.

It means they want to hear from you. You have a direct channel to them. Don't abuse it. Don't suddenly start flooding people's inboxes with get rich schemes. They signed up for you and your writing so make sure you deliver. Which leads us to the next question...

How Often To Mail

We've all experienced signing up for something on the internet, only to be bombarded with emails. Most of us immediately unsubscribe!

You need to maintain a fine balance between engaging with and not enraging your list. Even though people have voluntarily signed up to your mailing list, this doesn't give you the right to begin bombarding their inbox with emails every other day or worse.

Once a month is plenty, coinciding with your new blog post. If you are getting close to your book launch, increase the frequency because hey, it's exciting! Your new book is coming out. Maybe there's a discount! (It's called 'beating the drum' in internet marketing speak.)

TIP: Check out the Free Tools chapter for links to my favourite (and free) internet resources about email marketing. If you use the free Mailchimp, you'll find excellent resources to help you become an email expert in no time.

CHAPTER 13

The End of the Beginning...

So here we are at the end of How To Build Your Writer's Platform. You've learned why building your writer's platform is maybe the most important thing you can do if you are taking your self-published writing career seriously.

A writer's platform sets you up for success and if you put all the planks together well, you'll find it doesn't take up much of your time.

You've learned that planning your platform activity is crucial. If you map out your year in advance, you'll only need to spend at most an hour a week maintaining your writer's platform.

The best takeaway I can give you is to TAKE BABY STEPS. It's easy to get overwhelmed by all the detail of putting your writer's platform together. It can seem overwhelming at first - especially to writers who are uncomfortable using social media, self promotion and marketing.

One golden thread I've woven through this book is that you need to understand the basics of internet marketing to build a successful writer's platform. If you find marketing distasteful, then you will struggle building a platform and promoting your brand - YOU.

If you want to become an independent writer and publisher - an authorpreneur if you like - then you really do need to embrace these methods to sell your books.

Now, if you're lucky enough to get signed to a mainstream publisher, they will take care of some of this for you - but not always. And you won't have ultimate control. You'll be putting yourself in a much stronger position if you take the time to create, nurture and grow your own audience.

Take some time to dive into the basic internet marketing techniques. I recommend you model your platform on writers you admire, who are already writing in your genre. See what works for them. Sign up to their mailing lists, study their auto-responder emails. Learn from the emails they send you, from their blog posts, from their social media.

There's no need to reinvent the wheel for your platform. Do some research, find what seems to work and model your platform on that.

Building a writer's platform is a big task, but if you break it down into manageable chunks you'll be able to get it done. One baby step at a time. Remember, when you are building your writer's platform, there's no need to wait until every element is complete. You don't have to switch everything on at once. Just take incremental action and get the pieces of your platform in place, one plank at a time. If you try to do it all at once, you will get overwhelmed and most likely give up. If you follow my approach, and just work on your platform elements sequentially, you will amaze yourself at how much you can achieve in three short months.

The point of building your writer's platform is to promote your writing, build your mailing list and ultimately sell books. For brand new writers, you may be a couple of years away from self-publishing your first title. Building your platform now will be a great investment for you that will pay off when you finally publish. Imagine having a mailing list of a few thousand readers who are engaged with your writing and journey. It will make your book launch much more fun and profitable.

A final reminder. The purpose of building your writer's platform is to promote your writing and sell books, not to keep you away from your writing. With your writer's platform built and a media schedule in place, you'll find it's quite easy to maintain your entire platform for only 30 minutes a day. Once you've actually built your platform, you'll be in maintenance mode with plenty of time to focus on your writing.

If there is one message I'd like you to take away from this book, it's that the time to start building your writer's platform is yesterday. If you are serious about self-publishing and creating a career from writing, you simply must build your writer's platform. Every day you postpone is a day that you haven't grown your mailing list, which is the most valuable asset a self-published author can have. More valuable than anonymous likes on Facebook.

So, welcome to the world of the authorpreneur. Check out the Marketing Resources and Free Tools chapters for lists of resources and information about internet marketing, email copywriting and best practice.

So get cracking and good luck!

CHAPTER 14

Marketing Resources

I've referred often to internet marketing techniques. Here's a list of my online 'mentors' on the subject. I'm not affiliated with any of them. Sign up to their mailing lists, for valuable free information. If you want, sign up to their programs and dive deeper, but start with the free info while you set up your platform.

Internet Marketing

Jeff Walker has been running his Product Launch Formula workshops for over 15 years. I learned most of what I know about internet marketing from Jeff. His program runs once a year, but he provides a wealth of free marketing material. Check it out and sign up to his blog.

www.jeffwalker.com

Hubspot is an internet marketing behemoth. Aside from their paid or free platforms, there are hundreds of free eBooks on every aspect of internet marketing. You can even get a free CRM (customer relationship management) and form builder to link into your Wordpress pages. I've used Hubspot for many clients. You'll see when you search for anything on internet marketing, one of the top results will be Hubspot. That's because they're great!

www.hubspot.com

Copywriting

This is a huge subject. Writing copy for blog posts, webpages and social media is a very specialised area. Copyblogger is a great resource for writers in this field. You'll notice most articles you find when you search about copywriting will originate in Copyblogger. They provide lots of excellent free information to get you started on your journey.

www.copyblogger.com

Authorpreneurs

The best way to get started with your platform is by modelling it on those of self-published writers you admire. Here's a couple of mine:

Joanna Penn is a British writer and authorpreneur who has created a dual career as a self-published writer of paranormal thrillers, while also maintaining a comprehensive website of 'how to' guides.

www.thecreativepenn.com

www.jfpenn.com

American Jeff Goins writes non-fiction books in the motivation and writing niche. In a short time he's built an impressive platform that touches on all you need to know about being an authorpreneur.

www.goinswriter.com

Publishing

Australian publishing house Madhouse Media Publishing helps authors self-publish. Check out our blog 'The Write Stuff' and our regular podcast 'EBR - The Writers' Show' (of which yours truly is the host).

www.madhousemedia.com.au

www.ebookrevolutionpodcast.com

Affiliate Marketing

Affiliate Marketing is simply selling other people's products (usually by email) to your mailing list. You can earn a good percentage per sale. The key is don't overdo it, and only promote products that align with your personal brand. A great way to get started is:

www.shareasale.com

Chapter 15

Free Tools

The whole point of this book is to guide you to take action and build a platform with free tools that are already available. Here is a list of tools I've referred to throughout the book, and which I use myself every single day for my own platform and business marketing for clients.

Art and Graphics Tools

Canva is an incredible tool that lets you create professional looking graphics for any medium. One of the hardest things to learn if you are new to creating online graphics is the correct sizes demanded by each platform. Thankfully, Canva has you covered.

www.canva.com

https://www.canva.com/learn/12-common-image-formatting-mistakes-avoid-website/

Blog and Author Website Tools

I recommend Wordpress, as their free blog is so good. You can start free and upgrade to a paid domain name for a few dollars a month.

www.wordpress.com

Click Here for your Free Blog Planning Template from Madhouse Media Publishing.

Email Marketing and Auto-Responder Tools

Mailchimp's free plan gets you going. If you get over 1000 subscribers, you'll need to upgrade to a paid tier, but it's still good value.

www.mailchimp.com

Hubspot has a great free CRM and form builder, but the free version doesn't have an auto-responder. You can manually send a welcome email from Hubspot when you see someone sign up. If you're only getting a single sign-up every now and again, and don't mind logging in to send the email, Hubspot's free CRM has a lot of useful features.

www.hubspot.com

Google Docs and Sheets

This is an invaluable resource for writing copy, and keeping project maps and schedules. If you have a Gmail account, you already have access. If not, you'll need to create one. Well worth the effort.

https://www.google.com.au/docs/about/

Social Media Scheduling Tools

These tools take the work out of posting regular content. You just write or share content, and the scheduler automatically posts out to Twitter, Facebook, Instagram and LinkedIn. You can even design the schedule to suit, so if you only want to post to Instagram, or once a week, or 3 times a day - you're totally in control. I recommend these two platforms because they have a free entry-level version.

www.buffer.com

www.hootsuite.com

Social Media Content Calendar

Here is a free spreadsheet from Hubspot that helps you map out your media schedule. You can adapt it to help with your platform building as well (I use this myself).

https://blog.hubspot.com/blog/tabid/6307/bid/33415/the-social-media-publishing-schedule-every-marketer-needs-template.aspx

Useful Hashtags

Hashtags (#) are the secret sauce of social media engagement. When you hashtag a post, you are making it easy for new people to discover your post. By extension, they are discovering you and your platform.

When you start publishing content, you want to attract new visitors who may then sign up to your mailing list. It's good to have an understanding of how different platforms use hashtags differently.

A great resource is Best Hashtags (http://best-hashtags.com). This is an algorithm-driven list so it is always up-to-date. Try typing in 'writing' to find fellow writers and 'reading' to find readers. Remember, if you only hashtag writers, don't be surprised if no-one buys your book. You want readers. That said, it's good to have a mix.

About the Author

Geoff Hughes founded Madhouse Media Publishing in 2013 to help writers produce quality eBooks through effective internet marketing. He is passionate about self-published writers raising the bar on their professionalism.

He is an author, web designer and internet marketing professional, who has worked on marketing campaigns for some of the largest brands in Australia and South East Asia.

He is also the host of 'EBR - The Writers' Show' podcast - a monthly discussion with authors on the art, craft and business of writing.

Geoff lives in Port Macquarie, Australia and enjoys playing guitar that is maybe a little too loud, sailing, motorbikes, a good shiraz, conversation and good food.

Contact me @

Email: geoff@madhousemedia.com.au

Web: www.geoffhughes.com.au

Listen to 'EBR - The Writers' Show' podcast here:
www.ebookrevolutionpodcast.com

LinkedIn: linkedin.com/in/geoffhughes1

Twitter: twitter.com/geoffhughes01

Madhouse Media Publishing: www.madhousemedia.com.au

www.ingramcontent.com/pod-product-compliance
Lightning Source LLC
Chambersburg PA
CBHW020431010526
44118CB00010B/528